Pyramids and Temples

Jane Parker

RSVP

**RAINTREE
STECK-VAUGHN**

PUBLISHERS

The Steck-Vaughn Company

Austin, Texas

Published by Raintree Steck-Vaughn Publishers, an imprint of Steck-Vaughn Company

Library of Congress Cataloging-in-Publication Data

Parker, Jane, 1951-
      Pyramids and temples / Jane Parker; [illustrator, Kevin Maddison].
        p.   cm. — (Superstructures)
      Includes index.
      Summary: Provides a look at the various types of structures used in religious ceremonies by people throughout history, from caves and ancient pyramids to classical temples and modern cathedrals.
      ISBN 0-8172-4330-5
      1. Structural engineering — Juvenile literature.   2. Pyramids — Design and construction — Juvenile literature.   3. Temples — Design and construction — Juvenile literature.   4. Ziggurats — Design and construction — Juvenile literature. [1. Pyramids. 2. Temples. 3. Church buildings.]   I. Maddison, Kevin W., ill.   II. Title.   III. Series.
TA634.P36   1997
726 — dc20

                              96-4769
                              CIP   AC

Printed in Spain
Bound in the United States
1 2 3 4 5 6 7 8 9 0 LB 99 98 97 96

Designer: Frances McKay
Editor: Christine Hatt
Illustrator: Kevin Maddison
Picture researcher: Juliet Duff
Consultant: Anne Millard

Photographic credits
AKG London, p. 20.
Ancient Art and Architecture, p. 37.
Bridgeman Art Library, p. 34 Bibliothèque Nationale, Paris.
British Museum, London, p. 19.
Mary Evans Picture Library, p. 8.
Robert Harding Picture Library, p. 25.
Moroccan National Tourist Office, p. 39.
Science and Society Picture Library, p. 9.
© Superstock: cover
Zefa, p. 5.

Note to the reader:
Words in **bold** appear in the glossary on page 46.

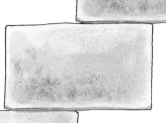

Contents

Pyramids and Temples

Some of the most impressive buildings in the world were created for worship. Many ancient peoples built spectacular temples to honor their gods and to thank them for the help and protection they gave.

Mud and straw

In earliest times, people worshiped in open spaces and natural caves. Later they began to build shelters for their sacred sites. In about 7000 BC, the people of Çatal Hüyük in Anatolia (modern-day Turkey) used bricks of mud and straw to construct their simple **shrines.** The Mesopotamians and the people of Central America also used mud bricks for their huge religious monuments.

Solid stone

Stone is the longest-lasting and most useful of all building materials. It can be shaped and decorated. It can be piled up in blocks, one on top of another. Stone can support great loads from above, as long as it is supported from below. About 5000 years ago, people first discovered how to cut and shape solid stone.

Early stone monuments

Soon, many new religious buildings were constructed from stone. In about 3600 BC, people began to build temples with stone walls on the island of Malta. About 1000 years later, the Egyptians piled up stone blocks to form pyramids. In England, the standing stones of Stonehenge were put in place between 2800 and 1500 BC.

◀ Step Pyramid Factfile

Height:	197 feet (60m)
Site:	Saqqara, Egypt
Built in:	About 2650 BC
Builder:	Imhotep for Pharaoh Zoser
Material:	Limestone blocks
Religion:	Ancient Egyptian

The Step Pyramid was one of the first large buildings ever made with cut stone blocks. It was built as a tomb for Pharaoh Zoser in about 2650 BC.

Chartres Cathedral Factfile

Height:	125 feet (38m)
Site:	Chartres, France
Built in:	1194-1220
Builder:	The Chartres Master
Material:	Carved stone
Religion:	Christian

Chartres Cathedral is a fine example of thirteenth-century Gothic architecture, famous for its stained glass.

From Greek to Gothic

Stone remained popular in later times. The civilizations of Greece and Rome used stone columns and domes to create temples with wide, open spaces inside. In the East, temples were cut into solid rock, or covered with stone carvings. From the twelfth century AD, stone was also used for the **Gothic** cathedrals of Europe.

Twentieth-century temples

Now, in the twentieth century, many different materials are used to construct religious buildings. But whichever material they choose, **architects** and builders try to make modern places of worship as striking and awe-inspiring as those of the past.

Angkor Wat Factfile ▶

Height:	213 feet (65m)
Site:	Cambodia
Built in:	About AD 1150
Builder:	King Suryavarman II
Material:	Carved sandstone
Religion:	Hindu and Buddhist

The largest temple in the world covers 1 square mile (2.5 sq km). It was built in the twelfth century AD at Angkor in Cambodia by the Khmer people.

STEP BY STEP

In this space on each double page we show you one stage in the construction of an imaginary pyramid. The sequence starts here and ends on page 21.

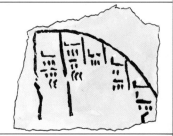

1 The pharaoh's architects draw diagrams and make calculations to work out the best size and shape for the new pyramid.

Egyptian Pyramids

The Ancient Egyptians settled on the banks of the Nile River about 10,000 years ago. Their earliest buildings were made of reeds and mud bricks, but by about 3000 BC they had learned to cut and shape stone. The people built pyramids for their dead kings and temples for their gods. These monuments are still among the world's most impressive structures.

Ancient Egyptian religion

The Ancient Egyptians worshiped many gods, and believed in life after death. They thought the spirit of Horus, falcon god and protector of Egypt, lived in their king, the pharaoh. When the pharaoh died, his body had to be preserved for the afterlife, so that he could watch over his people forever. So he needed a splendid tomb—a pyramid.

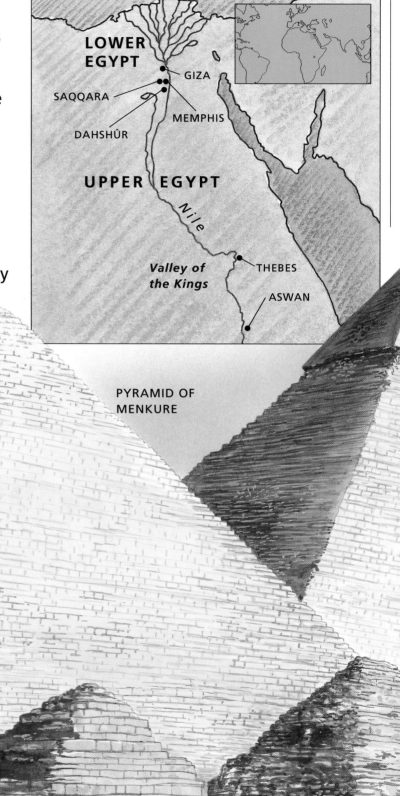

LOWER EGYPT

GIZA

SAQQARA

MEMPHIS

DAHSHÛR

UPPER EGYPT

Nile

Valley of the Kings

THEBES

ASWAN

PYRAMID OF MENKURE

QUEEN'S PYRAMIDS

Early government

Every year the Nile River flooded its banks, bringing fertile soil and water to the fields. The rich harvests of wheat, barley, fruits, and vegetables had to be stored and distributed to the people. This was done by the pharaoh's priests and officials, who carried out his orders. They were paid for by taxes, not in the form of money, but with crops and labor. During the floods, the young men could not work in the fields. This was when they paid their labor tax to the pharaoh—by building his pyramid. In return, they were given food, clothes, and lodging.

Pyramid complexes

Pyramids were usually part of a group of buildings called a pyramid complex. The buildings included a Valley Temple near the river and a **Mortuary Temple** at the pyramid. A **causeway** linked the two temples. The pharaoh's body was carried up the causeway for burial. The causeway walls were often decorated with scenes from the daily life of the people.

This statue is of Pharaoh Khufu, who ruled Egypt from about 2551-2528 BC. He ordered the Great Pyramid to be built at Giza, and was buried inside it.

GREAT PYRAMID
(PYRAMID OF KHUFU)

PYRAMID OF KHAFRE

7

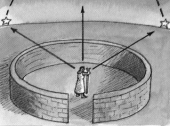

STEP BY STEP

2 Priests use the top of a wall to follow a star's east to west path. The midpoint is north, the way the pyramid faces.

Pyramid Shapes

Ordinary Egyptians were buried in desert sand. But pharaohs wanted impressive tombs. First they heaped sand and stones over their graves. These developed into mud-brick tombs called mastabas.

The first pyramid

The first pyramid, built in about 2650 BC, was a series of stone mastabas built one on top of the other—the Step Pyramid. Next, the Egyptians started to make straight-sided pyramids. By the time Khufu became pharaoh in about 2551 BC, Egyptian engineers had been building pyramids for 100 years. They quickly began work on his Great Pyramid at Giza.

MUMMIES
The pharaoh's body had to be preserved for the afterlife. This was done using a process called **mummification**. First the organs were removed, then the body was covered with natron, a chemical used to dry it. Next it was bandaged and placed in a coffin. Finally it was carried to the pyramid and put in a box called a **sarcophagus**. In the nineteenth century, many sarcophagi were opened (below).

MASTABAS
A mastaba was a rectangular tomb made of sun-dried mud bricks or stone. It marked the entrance to a burial chamber cut in the rock below. All the early pharaohs were buried beneath mastabas.

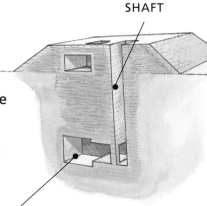

SHAFT

BURIAL CHAMBER

STEPPING UP
The Step Pyramid was built at Saqqara in about 2650 BC for Pharaoh Zoser. It had six steps of different sizes and was the first free-standing structure to be built of cut-stone blocks.

PHARAOH ZOSER

STEP PYRAMID

CHANGE OF PLAN
Pharaoh Snefru's Bent Pyramid was constructed at Dahshûr. When it was half finished, the architects became worried that it was too steep, so the sides were continued at a more gentle slope.

SNEFRU'S NAME IN HIEROGLYPHS

BENT PYRAMID

CASED IN STONE

Khafre, Khufu's son, built the second largest pyramid at Giza in about 2500 BC. Originally it was covered with white **limestone**, but now only the top stones remain. The limestone from all three Giza pyramids was stripped in the Middle Ages to build the city of Cairo.

PHARAOH KHAFRE

KHAFRE'S PYRAMID

FAST FINISH

The last of the three big pyramids at Giza was built for King Menkure in about 2490 BC. It is only half as high as the other two and was finished hurriedly when the king died.

PHARAOH MENKURE

MENKURE'S PYRAMID

TUTANKHAMEN'S TOMB

Eventually pharaohs stopped building pyramids. Instead they were buried in rock-cut chambers in the Valley of the Kings, near Thebes.

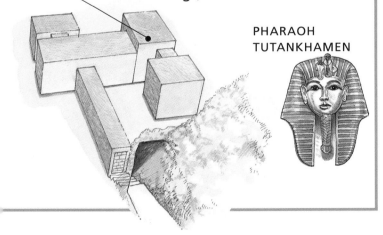

SARCOPHAGUS FOUND HERE

PHARAOH TUTANKHAMEN

THE FIRST ARCHITECT

The architect of Pharaoh Zoser's Step Pyramid was Imhotep. He shaped stone into neat, rectangular blocks that fit tightly together. When they were stacked on top of one another, the blocks supported each other, so that they did not fall over. First Imhotep built a stone mastaba, instead of the usual mud-brick ones. Then he tried putting several mastabas on top of one another. This formed the basic structure of all future pyramids. Imhotep also invented stone columns to hold up the roofs of temples around the pyramid.

*Imhotep was a gifted man who acted as the pharaoh's priest, magician, and **astrologer**.*

9

STEP BY STEP

3 The site is leveled and a grid of channels cut and filled with water. The rock is cut back to the water level, to make it flat.

Inside the Great Pyramid

The pyramid complex at Giza was one of the Seven Wonders of the Ancient World. The Great Pyramid, tomb of Pharaoh Khufu, was the first to be built there, in about 2550 BC. It is still the largest stone building in the world.

Facts and figures

Each side of the Great Pyramid measures 754 feet (230m). The pyramid was once 479 feet (146m) high and covered 13 acres (5.37ha). About 2.3 million blocks of stone were used to build it.

The Queen's Chamber

The entrance to the Great Pyramid is 60 feet (18m) above the ground. It leads down a tunnel, called the Descending Corridor, to an unfinished burial chamber under the pyramid. Another corridor leads to a room in the middle. This is called the Queen's Chamber, but it was probably originally intended for the pharaoh.

The King's Chamber

Above the passage leading to the Queen's Chamber is the entrance to the Grand Gallery. This huge, sloping room is 154 feet (47m) long and 28 feet (8.5m) high. At the top of the gallery is a short, narrow passageway with a tiny doorway at one end. This opens into the red **granite** King's Chamber. The chamber is 36 feet (11m) long, just over 16 feet (5m) wide, and almost 20 feet (6m) high. It contained the black granite sarcophagus of the pharaoh.

Supporting stones

Above the King's Chamber there are five granite slabs topped with two blocks leaning against each other to form a roof shape. These stones support the great weight pressing down from above. Two small shafts were made leading off the King's Chamber. These may have been designed to allow the pharaoh's soul to escape to heaven from the pyramid.

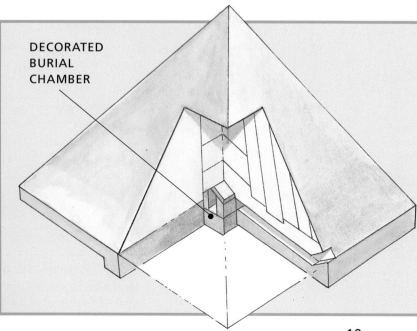

DECORATED BURIAL CHAMBER

THE PYRAMID OF UNAS
Pharaoh Khufu built his burial chamber inside the Great Pyramid. All other pyramids were built over burial chambers at ground level or cut into the rock below. This is the pyramid of Pharaoh Unas at Saqqara. Some of its stones were taken from Pharaoh Zoser's Step Pyramid, which was almost 300 years older. The Unas pyramid is now crumbling, but its decorated burial chamber is still well preserved.

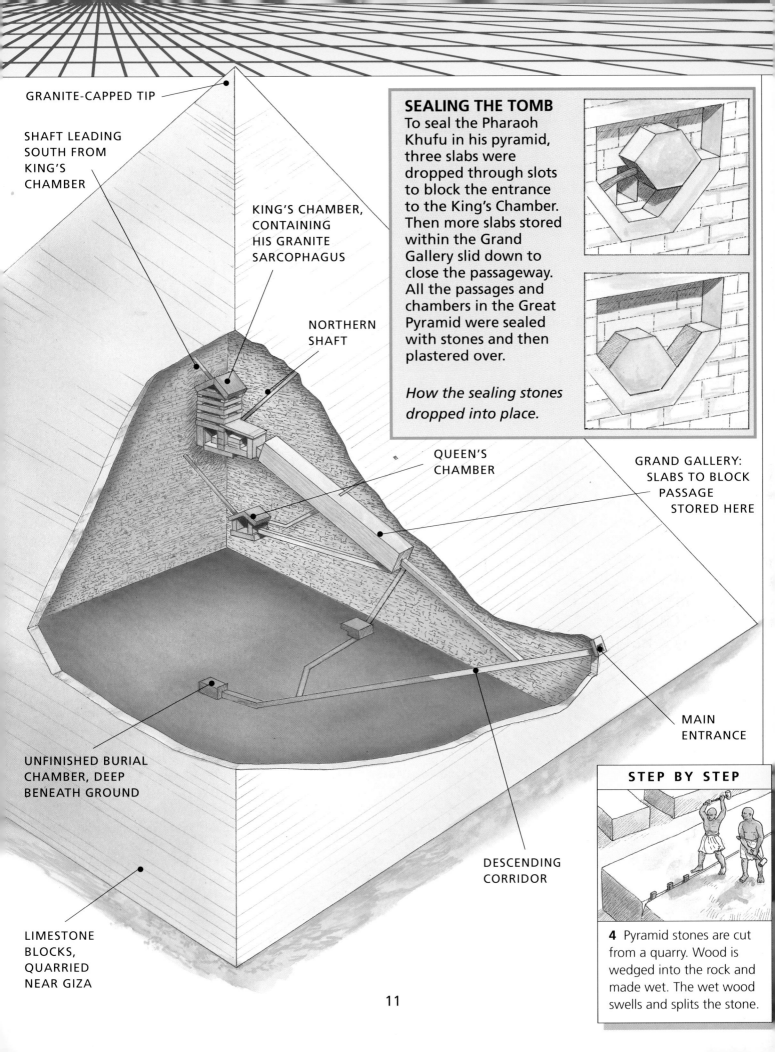

GRANITE-CAPPED TIP

SHAFT LEADING
SOUTH FROM
KING'S
CHAMBER

KING'S CHAMBER,
CONTAINING
HIS GRANITE
SARCOPHAGUS

NORTHERN
SHAFT

QUEEN'S
CHAMBER

UNFINISHED BURIAL
CHAMBER, DEEP
BENEATH GROUND

LIMESTONE
BLOCKS,
QUARRIED
NEAR GIZA

GRAND GALLERY:
SLABS TO BLOCK
PASSAGE
STORED HERE

MAIN
ENTRANCE

DESCENDING
CORRIDOR

SEALING THE TOMB
To seal the Pharaoh Khufu in his pyramid, three slabs were dropped through slots to block the entrance to the King's Chamber. Then more slabs stored within the Grand Gallery slid down to close the passageway. All the passages and chambers in the Great Pyramid were sealed with stones and then plastered over.

How the sealing stones dropped into place.

STEP BY STEP

4 Pyramid stones are cut from a quarry. Wood is wedged into the rock and made wet. The wet wood swells and splits the stone.

Building the Great Pyramid

Building the Great Pyramid was a complex process and needed careful planning by experts and hard work by thousands of men.

STEP 1 PREPARATIONS

The site of the Great Pyramid was chosen by priests, so that it faced the North Star. Then the sand was cleared away and the sides of the pyramid were measured. Finally, the site was leveled by filling a grid of channels with water, then cutting the rock to the water level. The drained channels were filled with pieces of stone.

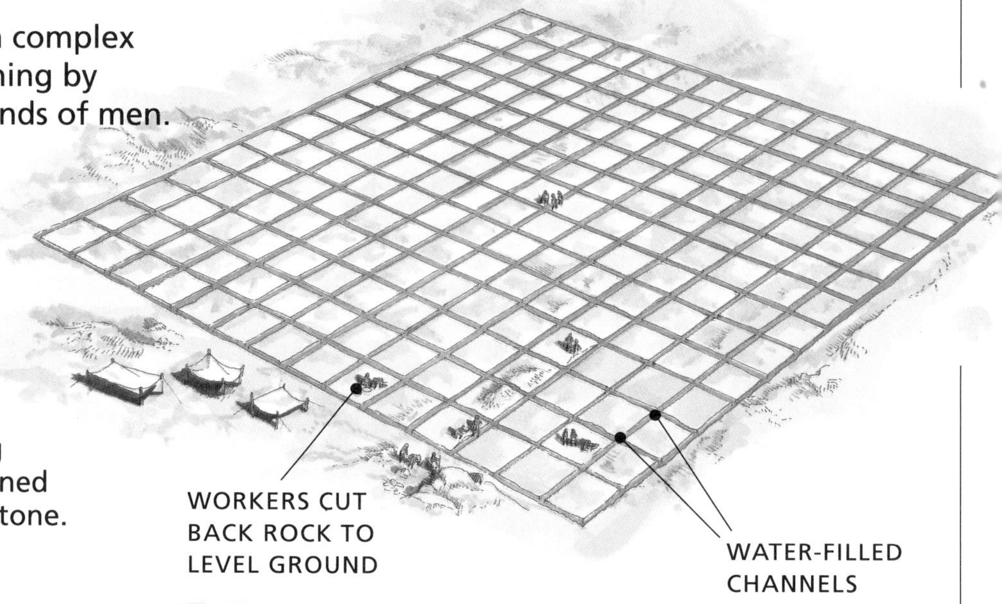

WORKERS CUT BACK ROCK TO LEVEL GROUND

WATER-FILLED CHANNELS

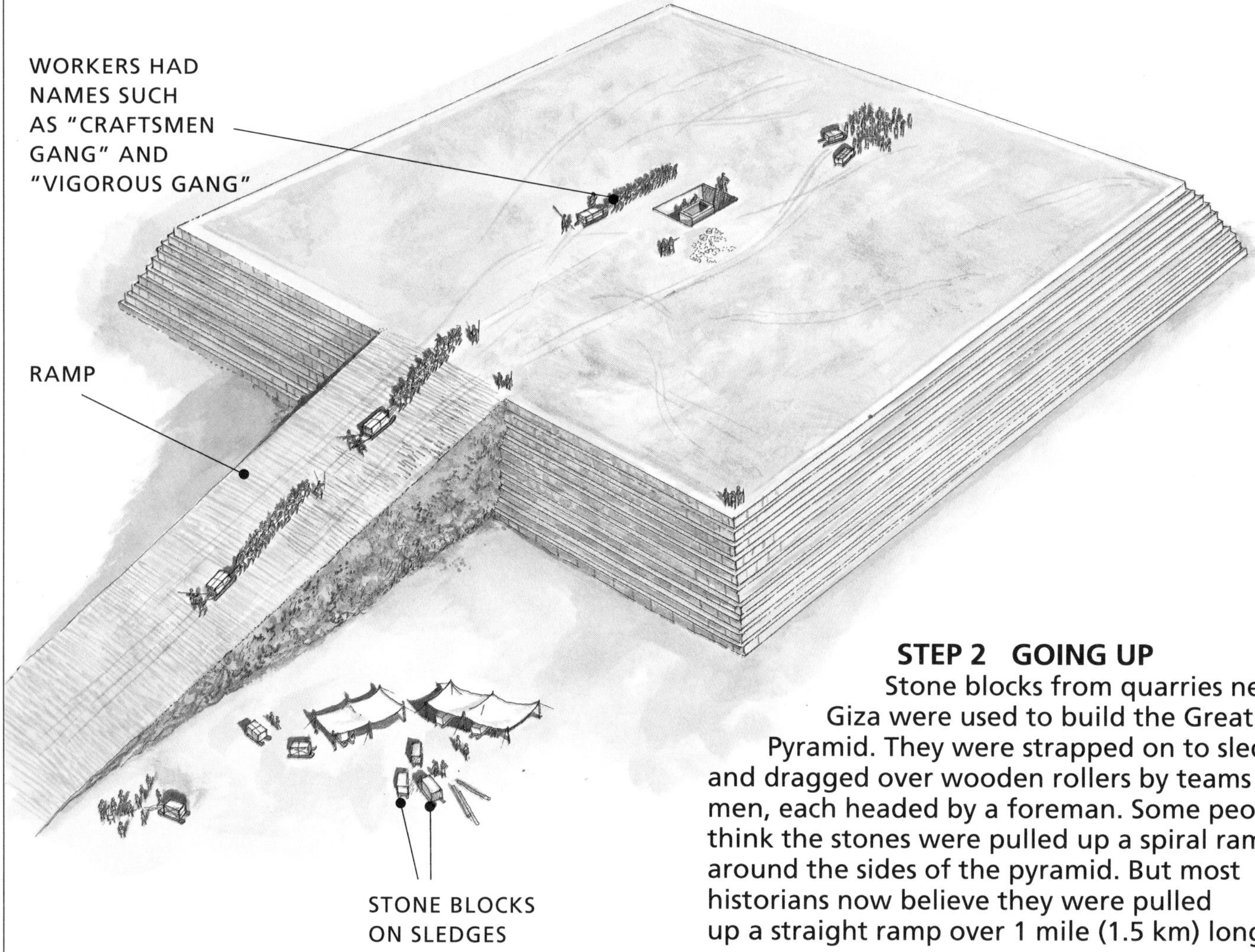

WORKERS HAD NAMES SUCH AS "CRAFTSMEN GANG" AND "VIGOROUS GANG"

RAMP

STONE BLOCKS ON SLEDGES

STEP 2   GOING UP

Stone blocks from quarries near Giza were used to build the Great Pyramid. They were strapped on to sledges and dragged over wooden rollers by teams of men, each headed by a foreman. Some people think the stones were pulled up a spiral ramp around the sides of the pyramid. But most historians now believe they were pulled up a straight ramp over 1 mile (1.5 km) long.

STEP 3   NEAR THE TOP

Pharaoh Khufu probably visited the site regularly with his building experts. They checked the angles of the sides with a **plumb line,** to make sure they were accurate. Priests visited too, to say prayers to bless the work. Spaces were left between the stones for the passageways. Granite blocks were brought to line the chambers.

SUPPORTING STONES ABOVE KING'S CHAMBER

LAYERS OF STONE BLOCKS

GRANITE CAPSTONE

STEP 4   FINISHING OFF

The 200 layers of blocks were topped by a granite **capstone.** Then the pyramid was covered from top to bottom with limestone facing stones. These were shaped very accurately so that they would fit together tightly.

STEP BY STEP

5 The stone blocks are squared and made smooth. Then men use levers, ropes, and sledges on rollers to move them.

Ziggurats

The Sumerians, another early civilization, lived a few hundred miles (km) to the east of Egypt, in Mesopotamia (now Iraq). They farmed the fertile land between the Tigris and Euphrates rivers. The area was divided into **city-states**, and the people believed a different god watched over each one. Temples were built on top of huge platforms, called ziggurats, so that everyone could see them. The ziggurats had terraces and grand staircases. Sumerians believed gods used the staircases to walk between Earth and their home in heaven.

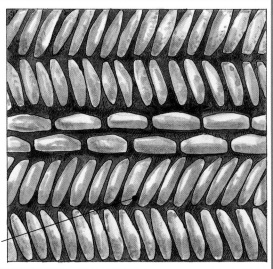

WORKERS BUILDING TEMPLE

MUD-BRICK TERRACES

BUILDING BRICKS

To build their ziggurats, the Sumerians made loaf-shaped bricks from mud mixed with straw. The mixture was packed into **molds** to shape it. Then the molds were removed and the bricks dried in the hot sun. The bricks were often arranged in a herringbone pattern. To stick them together, Sumerians used mud or bitumen, a black, oily substance that oozed up through the hot desert sands.

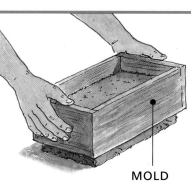

MOLD

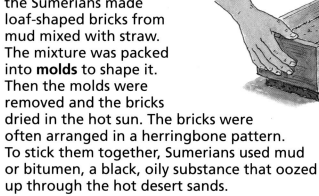

HERRINGBONE BRICK PATTERN

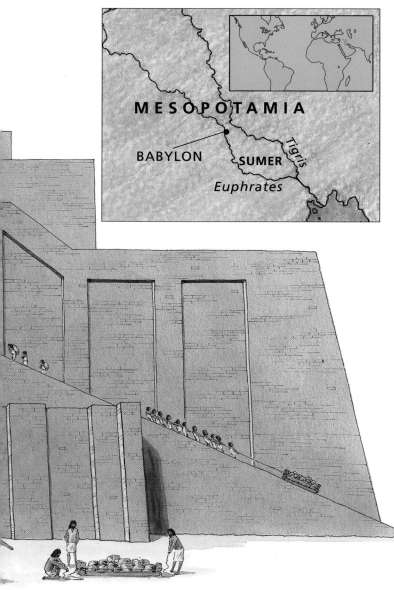

Biblical ziggurats

The Babylonians lived in Mesopotamia after the Sumerians. Nebuchadrezzar was one of their kings. He built a ziggurat with a temple dedicated to the god **Marduk** on the top. This was probably the Tower of Babel mentioned in the Bible. In the story, men build the tower to reach heaven, but God punishes them by making them all speak different languages.

The Hanging Gardens

Nebuchadrezzar also built the Hanging Gardens of Babylon, for his queen, Amytis. This ziggurat-like building had trees and plants along its terraces. Like the Great Pyramid of Giza, it was one of the Seven Wonders of the Ancient World.

Ur-Nammu (right) was king of the Sumerian city of Ur in 2100 BC. He built a 68 foot- (21m-) high ziggurat (left) for the Moon god, Nanna. Priests carried food and offerings for the god up and down the central steps daily.

THEN AND NOW

In about 2100 BC, Ur was an extremely powerful city, and its beautifully decorated ziggurat towered above the busy streets. But the city was invaded in 2000 BC and gradually became less important. In the fourth century BC, it was finally abandoned. King Ur-Nammu's ziggurat has been repaired many times since then and the lowest of its three terraces (above) still survives today—more than 4000 years after it was first built by the people of ancient Sumer.

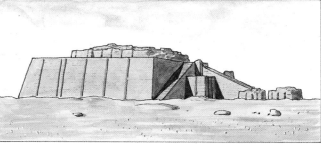

6 Next, men drag the sledges to the pyramid and pull the stones up a massive ramp more than 1 mile (1.5km) long.

American Pyramids

There were many great civilizations in Mexico and Central America before it was explored by the Spanish in the sixteenth century. The peoples of the region believed that their gods would only be strong enough to protect the land and its people if they received regular offerings of human blood. So they built huge pyramid temples for human sacrifice.

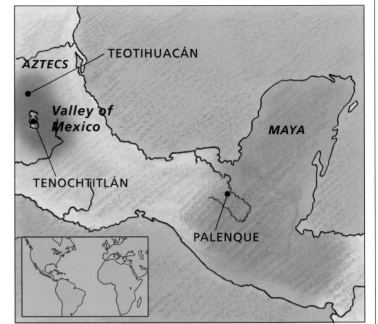

The earliest peoples in Mexico built terraces on hillsides for worship. Then they built mounds for ceremonies. This one is in the Valley of Mexico.

Maya pyramids

The Maya civilization existed from about 2000 BC to the time of the Spanish conquest. The people were **astronomers** and mathematicians. They used writing and had an accurate calendar. Their great, stepped pyramids were built of rubble and earth, covered with cut stone blocks. The temples on top were decorated with **friezes** in bright colors. New, bigger pyramids were built over the old ones.

This Maya death mask (right) is carved from jade, a symbol of life and immortality. It was buried under the temple at Palenque.

The Maya Temple of the Inscriptions at Palenque was built over the tomb of King Pacal, who ruled from AD 615 to 683.

16

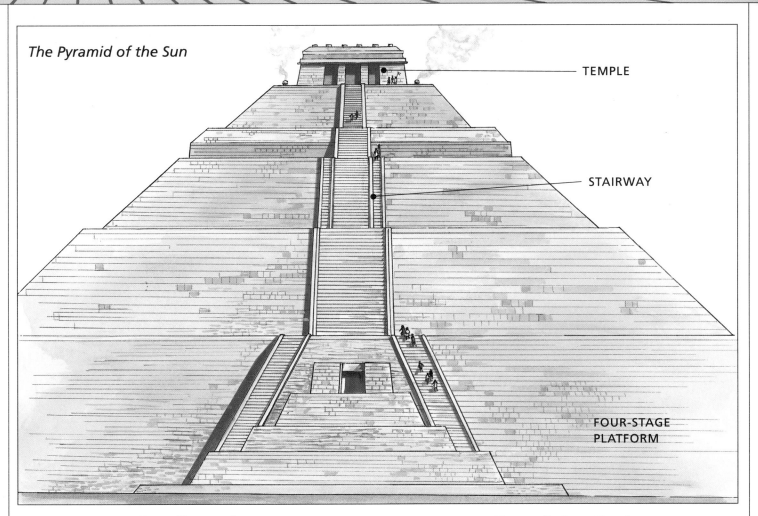

The Pyramid of the Sun

TEMPLE

STAIRWAY

FOUR-STAGE
PLATFORM

Teotihuacán

Teotihuacán was built 2,000 years ago, near the site of modern-day Mexico City. At that time it was one of the largest cities in the world. Its roads and buildings were laid out in a grid pattern. Towering over the palaces, temples, and market places were two great pyramids. These were the Pyramids of the Moon and the Sun.

Most Mexican peoples built their pyramids by making mounds of rubble. Then they laid similarly shaped stone blocks on the outside.

City of the Gods

The Pyramid of the Sun covered as large an area as the Great Pyramid in Egypt, although the building was only half as high. It was made of 2.5 million tons of sun-dried mud bricks. The Aztecs of the fifteenth and sixteenth centuries AD thought Teotihuacán had been built by the gods. The Aztecs were the last of the great Mexican civilizations. They made pilgrimages to this pyramid from their nearby capital city, Tenochtitlán.

STEP BY STEP

7 A space is left near the center of the pyramid for the burial chamber. The pharaoh's sarcophagus is lowered in from above.

Cave Worship

People of the distant past used caves to shelter from bad weather and to protect themselves from wild animals. It may have been in caves, with firelight flickering on the walls, that people first started to wonder about life and death and to tell stories of the gods.

Powerful pictures

About 30,000 years ago, people started to paint the walls of caves with pictures of the animals they hunted for food. These paintings, deep inside caves such as the one at Lascaux in France, may have been intended to make the hunters successful. The artists had only the dim light of simple oil lamps to see their work.

The rock-cut temple of Pharaoh Ramses II at Abu Simbel on the Nile River. Twice a year, the Sun shines directly through the entrance, to light up the statues of four gods inside.

ONE OF FOUR STATUES GUARDING ENTRANCE

STATUES LINING INSIDE OF TEMPLE

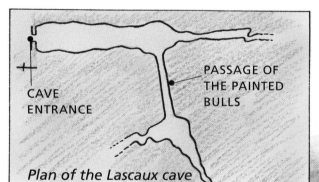

PASSAGE OF THE PAINTED BULLS

CAVE ENTRANCE

Plan of the Lascaux cave

*The wall paintings in the cave of Lascaux, south-west France, date from about 15,000 years ago, during the **Ice Age**. Most show animals, and one passage is covered with paintings of running bulls.*

Four 68 foot- (21m-) high statues of Pharaoh Ramses II guard the front of the temple.

ENTRANCE STATUES SEEN FROM FRONT

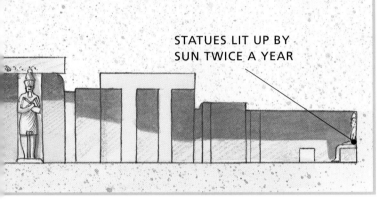

STATUES LIT UP BY SUN TWICE A YEAR

*The Caves of the Thousand Buddhas at Tun-huang in China are filled with **gilded** statues of the Buddha set in places specially cut into the rock.*

Abu Simbel

The temple of Pharaoh Ramses II at Abu Simbel is a human-made cave, cut into cliffs on the banks of the Nile in about 1250 BC. The temple is lined with pillars and divided into the same rooms as free-standing temples. In 1964, the temple was cut into pieces and rebuilt 200 feet (61m) higher, to protect it from the rising waters caused by the newly built Aswan Dam.

Hindu and Buddhist caves

Ancient Hindus and Buddhists worshiped in huge, human-made caves called *chaitya*. Inside, massive pillars and vaults are carved into the rock to make the caves look like free-standing buildings. At Ajanta in western India there are 29 rock-cut temples, some over 2000 years old. The walls are covered with paintings and sculptures of scenes from the life of the **Buddha**. Other Indian rock temples, at Elephanta and Ellora, are decorated with carvings of Hindu gods and their lives.

Silk Road Buddhas

The Caves of the Thousand Buddhas were built in the fourth century AD at Tun-huang on the famous trade route called the Silk Road. They held many sacred sculptures and manuscripts. At Bemian, Afghanistan, Buddhist monasteries and temples were cut into the cliffs. The world's tallest stone sculpture, a 174 foot- (53m-) high Buddha, is here.

STEP BY STEP

8 A huge granite capstone is laid at the top of the pyramid. The rest of the pyramid is covered with polished white limestone.

Open-Air Worship

Many ancient peoples worshiped in the open air, where they could watch the stars and planets and be close to their nature gods. Some worshiped on hilltops, where they often built stone pillars. Others preferred forest sites. Some prayed near rivers, often throwing in offerings such as weapons and jewelry. Others marked their sacred sites by building **earthworks** or erecting standing stones.

Sacred site

At Externsteine in Germany, strangely shaped rock pillars tower above the trees. The site has been sacred to people since the **Stone Age**. Over thousands of years, chapels and shrines with windows and doors have been cut into the rocks. The walls are carved with serpents, which perhaps symbolized the energy from the Earth that people believed they could feel here. Christians later carved scenes from the Bible over the **pagan** characters.

The weird rock formations at Externsteine in Germany were originally carved by wind and rain. But people have added steps, caves, altars, and religious symbols to nature's work.

ALTAR STONE

HEEL STONE

The main stone circles of Stonehenge (right) were part of a much larger site (above) with the massive Heel Stone at its entrance.

SANDSTONE SARSENS

Stonehenge

Men started building Stonehenge on Salisbury Plain in England about 5000 years ago. It began as an earthwork—a circular ditch and bank. The gigantic Heel Stone marked the entrance. Two rings of **bluestones** were erected in the earthwork, then two rings of **sarsens**. Some bluestones were later arranged in a horseshoe shape around the altar.

Nature worship

On the first day of summer, June 21, the rising Sun shines across the top of the Heel Stone, through the opening of the horseshoe and onto the altar stone. The people of Stonehenge may have used this monument to mark the changing seasons.

THE GREAT SERPENT MOUND

Earth mounds have been constructed by many peoples. The Great Serpent Mound in Ohio is 1,330 feet (405m) long. It may have been used as a site for worship. The serpent shape can only be seen from the air, so nobody knows how ancient peoples were able to design it.

Specially shaped joints were used to attach **lintels** *to the top of the sarsen stones.*

BLUESTONES

LINTELS

STEP BY STEP

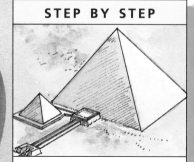

9 The Mortuary Temple, the Valley Temple, and the causeway that links them complete the great pyramid complex.

Early Temples

In about 3600 BC, the **Bronze Age** people of Malta and Gozo, islands in the Mediterranean, began to build some of the earliest stone temples. The people probably worshiped a mother goddess. They believed she brought life from the Earth each spring. Walls of standing stones surrounded the temples, and outside there were courtyards for ceremonies.

Animal sacrifices

Inside the temples were curved chambers, called **apses**, where animal sacrifices were made. The walls were carved with spiritual symbols, such as spirals and snakes. Bodies buried beneath the temples were curled into the shape of babies in the womb, waiting to be born again.

*The diagram (far right) shows the two Ggantija Temples , the Northern and the Southern, in Gozo. They are built in a **trefoil** pattern joined by paved corridors. Both had wide entrances, which were originally roofed with stone slabs. This is the entrance to the Northern Temple (right).*

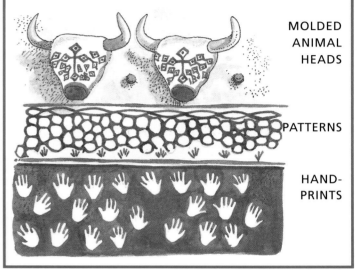

ÇATAL HÜYÜK
Çatal Hüyük in Turkey was one of the first towns in the world. Some of its mud-brick buildings were shrines to a mother goddess. Their inside walls were decorated with patterns, handprints and molded animal heads. The dead were buried under the floors of these shrines.

MOLDED ANIMAL HEADS

PATTERNS

HAND-PRINTS

ROOFED HYPOSTYLE HALL

PERISTYLE HALL
OPEN TO SKY

A typical Egyptian temple. Two huge halls led to the sanctuary, which contained a shrine where the god was believed to live.

SANCTUARY

Egyptian temples

The first Ancient Egyptians built shelters for their gods from bundles of **papyrus** reeds that grew in the swamps along the banks of the Nile River. At first these shelters were simple shrines, each with a porch supported by pillars and a small, fenced **forecourt**. When these fragile buildings were rebuilt with stronger materials, they became larger and more elaborate. But the layout remained basically the same.

WOOD DOORS WERE HERE

PYLONS OR HUGE GATEWAYS GUARD ENTRANCE

SOUTHERN TEMPLE

NORTHERN TEMPLE

Temple layout

Decorated pylons supported the heavy doors to the open **peristyle hall** of a temple. From there, steps led up to the roofed **hypostyle hall** and on to a sanctuary containing the god's statue. Avenues were lined with **sphinxes** and courtyards decorated with **obelisks.** These led to the temples that always faced the Nile.

STEP BY STEP

In this space on each double page we show you one stage in the construction of an imaginary cathedral. The sequence starts here and ends on page 39.

1 Plans are drawn up by the architect and shown to the bishop and **chapter**. They decide when the building can begin.

23

Eastern Temples

Hinduism began about 5000 years ago in India, among the people of one of the world's earliest civilizations. Hindu people worship many gods, among them Brahma, Vishnu, and Shiva, and their wives, the goddesses Sarasvati, Lakshmi, and Kali. The first Hindu temples were carved into rock faces, but in about AD 700, Hindus began to build freestanding temples.

Dark shrines

A Hindu temple is dedicated to one god or goddess. Inside, a series of pillared halls and corridors leads to a dark shrine where the god's statue is kept. A temple tower is built over the shrine. People visit temples to make offerings to their favorite gods, but there are no formal services like those in churches. Hindus believe that the gods live wherever their statues are kept. So most people worship at shrines in their homes.

*The seventeenth-century temple complex of the goddess Minakshi towers above the city of Madurai in India. Its **gopurams** (gateways) are covered with fine carvings.*

GOPURAMS

TEMPLE TANK FOR WORSHIPERS TO BATHE IN

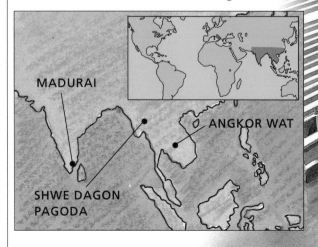

MADURAI

ANGKOR WAT

SHWE DAGON PAGODA

24

Shwe Dagon Pagoda

The Shwe Dagon Pagoda is near Rangoon in Myanmar (formerly known as Burma). It has been holy since the sixth century BC, when the Buddha gave various **mementos** to two Burmese merchants there. In the fifteenth century, a **pagoda** was built to house the sacred objects, and the rulers of Burma have built bigger and better shrines for them ever since.

Golden steeple

King Hsinbyushin built the present temple in 1768. His workmen used 10 million bricks and 100,000 brass screws. The temple covers 14 acres (5.6ha) and contains 3,538 bells. The golden dome, called a **stupa**, is covered with new gold leaf every 20 years. This is paid for by **pilgrims** and visitors. Gold and silver bells hang from the gem-encrusted spire on top.

*The magnificent Shwe Dagon Pagoda. The marble terraces around the stupa are lined with tiny shrines called **tazoungs**, each with its own pagoda on top.*

TAZOUNG
PAGODA

ANGKOR WAT

Angkor in Cambodia was the capital of the Khmer empire about 1000 years ago. About 600,000 people lived there in an area of 75 square miles (195 sq km). When it was rediscovered in 1850 by the French missionary Father Charles-Emile Bouillevaux, its houses and palaces had disappeared beneath the jungle trees. The most impressive of the 100 temples, called *wats*, is the tomb of King Suryavarman II. Covering 1 square mile (2.5 sq km), it is the largest temple in the world.

The lotus-blossom towers of Angkor Wat, built of brick and stone, rise 213 feet (65m) above the forest floor.

STEP BY STEP

2 Stone masons begin to cut the stone blocks for the walls, piers, and flying buttresses of the new cathedral.

Greek Temples

The Ancient Greeks had a great influence on modern European civilization. Their inquiring minds led them to write great works of literature and to look at the world around them in a scientific way.

The Doric Temple of the goddess Aphaia was built on the Greek island of Aegina in 490 BC. Like all Greek temples, it was made of rows of columns supporting beams that held up the roof.

DECORATIVE FIGURES

PEDIMENT DECORATED WITH BATTLE SCENES

CAPITAL

SHAFT

DORIC COLUMNS

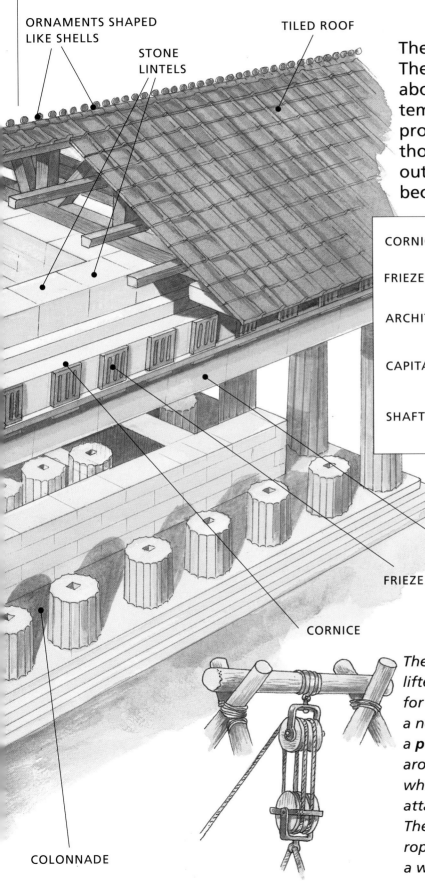

ORNAMENTS SHAPED
LIKE SHELLS

STONE
LINTELS

TILED ROOF

Inside and outside

The Greeks were great architects, too. They believed the most important thing about their buildings, especially their temples, was the appearance. They used proportions and decorations that they thought would please the gods. The outside was as important as the inside because people worshiped outside.

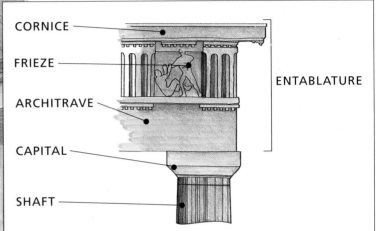

CORNICE

FRIEZE

ARCHITRAVE

ENTABLATURE

CAPITAL

SHAFT

*The Ancient Greeks designed three architectural styles, called **orders**. The Doric order (above) appeared in about 600 BC and was the first and the plainest. The Ionic order featured carved scrolls. The Corinthian order used leaves.*

ARCHITRAVE

FRIEZE

CORNICE

*The Ancient Greeks lifted the stone blocks for their temples using a new invention called a **pulley**. A rope passed around one or more wheels and was attached to each block. The other end of the rope was pulled using a winding wheel.*

COLONNADE

STEP BY STEP

3 Laborers dig holes for the foundations and the **crypt**. These are lined with gravel. Then stone blocks are laid on the top.

Roman Temples

The Ancient Romans were great builders and engineers, as well as soldiers. But they were not so much inventors as improvers. They wanted to worship their many gods inside their temples as well as outside, so they needed large, covered spaces. To build these, they improved a structure that had probably been invented by the Egyptians or Sumerians thousands of years earlier — the arch.

Roman arches

An arch does not sag in the middle as a beam does. This is because the weight of the building above presses down on each wedge-shaped stone, which then pushes against and supports the stone next to it. So arches can span larger spaces than beams. The greatest achievement of Roman arch-building was the dome, a form of circular arch.

PORCH

PEDIMENT

THE MAISON CARRÉE

CORINTHIAN COLUMNS

One of the best preserved of all Roman temples is the Maison Carrée in Nîmes, France. It was built in 19 BC by Marcus Agrippa, a son-in-law of Emperor Augustus. The Romans borrowed most of their decorative styles from the Greek orders, especially the Corinthian. Roman columns were often more elaborate.

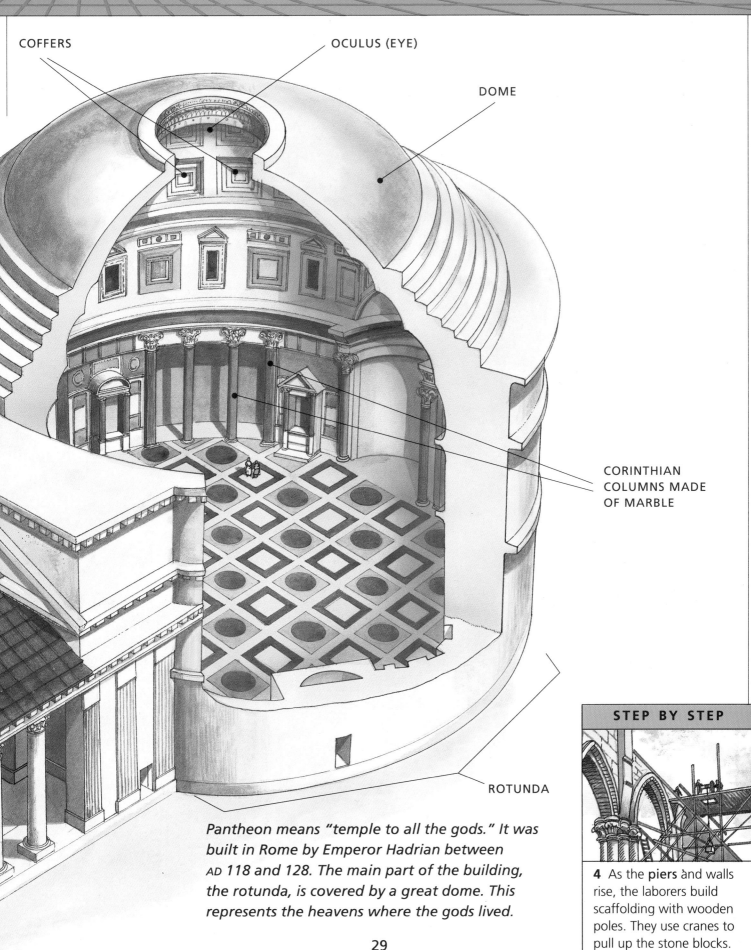

COFFERS

OCULUS (EYE)

DOME

CORINTHIAN COLUMNS MADE OF MARBLE

ROTUNDA

Pantheon means "temple to all the gods." It was built in Rome by Emperor Hadrian between AD 118 and 128. The main part of the building, the rotunda, is covered by a great dome. This represents the heavens where the gods lived.

STEP BY STEP

4 As the **piers** and walls rise, the laborers build scaffolding with wooden poles. They use cranes to pull up the stone blocks.

Building Roman Temples

The Romans developed methods and materials to help them build temples throughout their empire. Most temples were rectangular. But the Pantheon, the greatest achievement of Roman builders, was circular. It took ten years to build.

Concrete walls

The rotunda walls were built by pouring concrete between rows of bricks. Two stories of arched corridors were built into the walls. The outside was covered with concrete and the inside decorated with marble. The columns of the porch were topped with arches to hold up the roof.

CONCRETE

Concrete is a mixture of **cement, aggregate**, or rubble, and water. The cement the Romans used was a volcanic dust called *pozzolana* mixed with **lime**. The aggregate they used depended on the job. Stone rubble was used for strength, **pumice** and broken pots for lightness. Earlier peoples had used cement to hold stones and bricks together, but the Romans perfected the use of concrete as a building material in its own right.

BUILDING AN ARCH

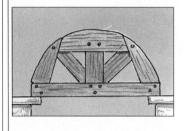

*1 A wooden frame, called a **centering**, is built on scaffolding between piers, the supports on either side of the arch.*

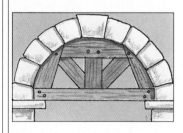

*2 Wedge-shaped stones, or **voussoirs**, are laid over the frame, from the bottom to the top. Each one is carefully cemented into place.*

*3 As soon as the central voussoir, or **keystone**, is in place, the arch supports itself and the frame is removed. The arch is complete.*

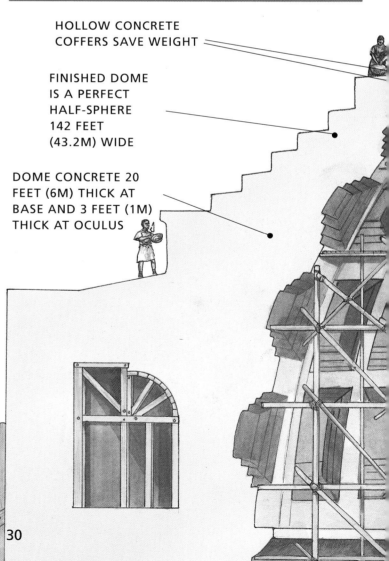

HOLLOW CONCRETE COFFERS SAVE WEIGHT

FINISHED DOME IS A PERFECT HALF-SPHERE 142 FEET (43.2M) WIDE

DOME CONCRETE 20 FEET (6M) THICK AT BASE AND 3 FEET (1M) THICK AT OCULUS

30

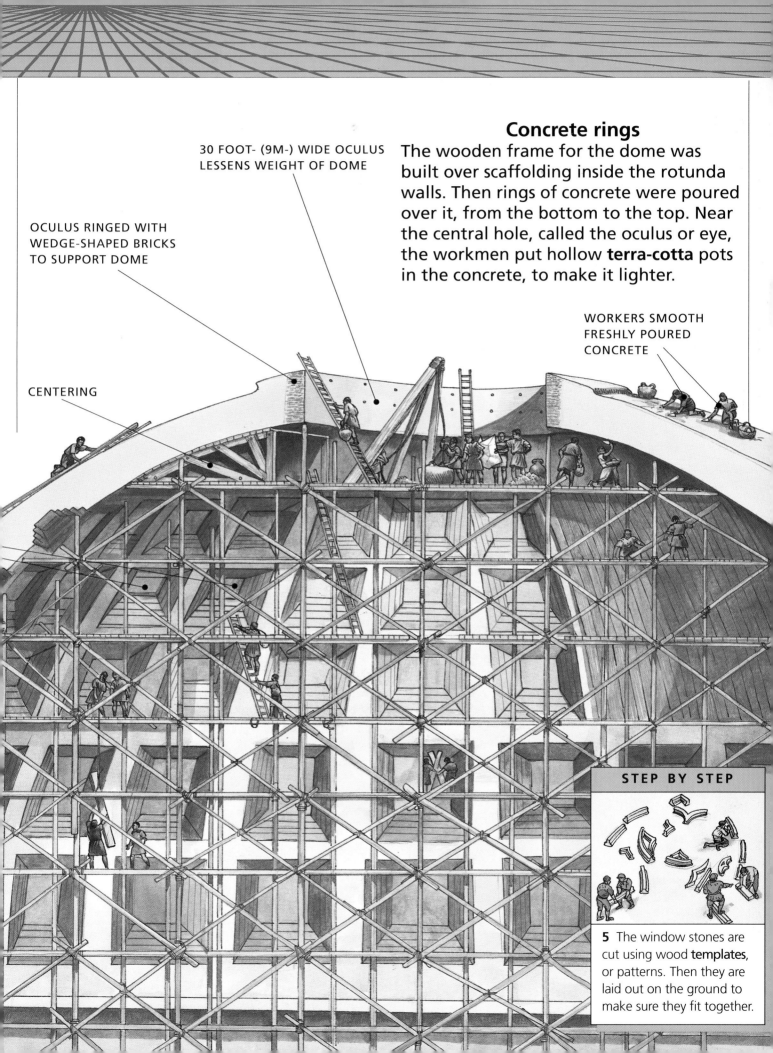

30 FOOT- (9M-) WIDE OCULUS
LESSENS WEIGHT OF DOME

OCULUS RINGED WITH
WEDGE-SHAPED BRICKS
TO SUPPORT DOME

CENTERING

Concrete rings

The wooden frame for the dome was built over scaffolding inside the rotunda walls. Then rings of concrete were poured over it, from the bottom to the top. Near the central hole, called the oculus or eye, the workmen put hollow **terra-cotta** pots in the concrete, to make it lighter.

WORKERS SMOOTH
FRESHLY POURED
CONCRETE

STEP BY STEP

5 The window stones are cut using wood **templates**, or patterns. Then they are laid out on the ground to make sure they fit together.

Early Churches

The first Christians worshiped in each other's houses, gathering quietly together to eat ceremonial meals. They did not need churches because there were only a few of them, and they had to hide from **persecution** by the Romans.

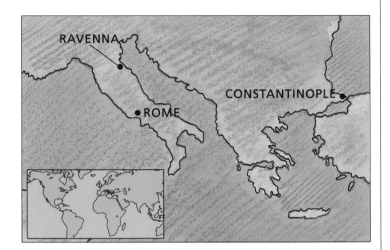

Emperor Constantine

In AD 313, Emperor Constantine made Christianity legal. In 391, it became the official religion of the Roman Empire. Constantine set up his new capital in Byzantium, in modern-day Turkey. He called it Constantinople, now Istanbul. The new Christians did not want to use the old pagan temples for worship, so they used the town halls, called **basilicas**.

Inside a basilica

Basilicas had narrow central **naves** with high wooden roofs held up by two rows of columns and arches. Aisles ran down either side. These had lower roofs and thick walls. The altar was placed in a semicircular apse at one end. This became the basic plan for all Christian churches.

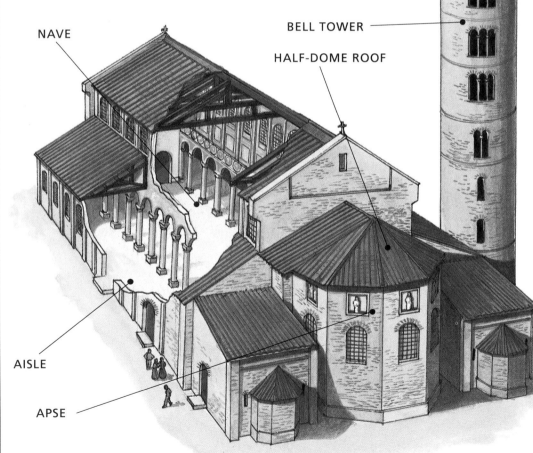

NAVE

BELL TOWER

HALF-DOME ROOF

AISLE

APSE

The basilica of Sant' Apollinare in Classe, Ravenna, Italy was built in AD 539 by Emperor Justinian. Like most basilicas, it has a single nave and two side aisles. The apse at one end has a half-dome roof. The round bell tower is one of the earliest ever built.

Hagia Sophia

In AD 532 Emperor Justinian decided to erect the most magnificent cathedral ever built. He chose the site of Constantine's ruined church in the great city of Constantinople. He wanted to combine the long nave of the basilicas with the high domes of Roman temples to create a vast, airy, light-filled space.

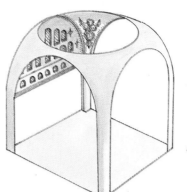

*The great weight of Hagia Sophia's domes had to be supported. This was done by structures called **pendentives**. These are curved arches that transfer the weight from the round base of the dome down through four columns to the ground.*

TWIN HALF DOMES

ONE OF FOUR SUPPORTING COLUMNS

RING OF WINDOWS

CENTRAL SQUARE MEASURES JUST OVER 98 FEET (30M) ALONG EACH SIDE

Support system

Justinian supervised the 10,000 men and 100 **overseers** himself. They built the church in only five years. The granite and brick nave is 200 feet (60m) long and 100 feet (30m) wide, decorated with marble, **mosaics**, and gold. The dome is circled with windows and stands on four great columns. It is supported by two half domes, which are supported by smaller half domes, aisles, and walls of windows.

Hagia Sophia still stands after centuries of battles and earthquakes. It was originally a church, became a mosque in 1453, and since 1935 has been a museum.

Gothic Cathedrals

During the early Middle Ages, most Christian churches built in Europe were dark, somewhat gloomy places. But in the twelfth century, a religious revival began, and a new style of building, called Gothic architecture, grew up. Over the next 400 years, many beautiful churches and cathedrals were built in this style.

Cathedrals of light

The people of Europe wanted to worship in buildings where their hearts and minds would be lifted toward heaven. The new Gothic churches had tall, pointed arches and high ceilings with **rib vaults**, supported by **flying buttresses**. Huge, brightly colored stained glass windows were set into thin walls. These windows showed scenes from the Bible.

This fifteenth-century painting shows medieval masons at work cutting, shaping, and carving stone. The best masons traveled around the cities of Europe, using their skills on many cathedrals.

NORTH SPIRE

SOUTH SPIRE

ROYAL PORTAL (DOORWAY OR PORCH)

Bigger and better

Gothic cathedrals sprang up all over Europe. The people of each city wanted to build a bigger and better one than ever before to thank God for his blessings — and to impress neighboring cities. Cathedral building sites even became tourist attractions for visitors.

The people's cathedrals

Everyone helped. The rich provided the money. The bishop and clergy checked the architect's plans. Masons and sculptors, carpenters, blacksmiths, and glassmakers did the skilled work, and apprentices helped them. Laborers lifted materials, dug holes, and mixed cement. The city's shops and inns provided food, drink, lodging, and clothes.

One of the most magnificent of all Gothic cathedrals is Chartres Cathedral in northern France. It was built between 1194 and 1230, and is the sixth church on the same site. The main cathedral building can hold 18,000 people.

NAVE 440 FEET (134M) LONG AND 52 FEET (16M) WIDE

VAULTS 125 FEET (38M) HIGH

APSE

ONE OF FIVE SMALL CHAPELS

ROSE WINDOW

SOUTH PORCH

LANCET WINDOW (HIGH NARROW WINDOW)

FLYING BUTTRESS

STEP BY STEP

7 The triangular roof **trusses** are made on the ground, then taken apart, hoisted into position with a crane and reassembled.

Building Gothic Cathedrals

The architects and masons of Europe's great Gothic cathedrals gradually devised new construction techniques to create their beautiful buildings.

Fear of fire

So many churches had been destroyed by fire that Gothic architects wanted to build their ceiling vaults from stone instead of wood. But vaults, like all arches, pushed their supporting walls outwards. Solid walls and buttresses strong enough to withstand the push of the stone would have used huge amounts of materials and labor. They would also have been too heavy and ugly for the airy Gothic design.

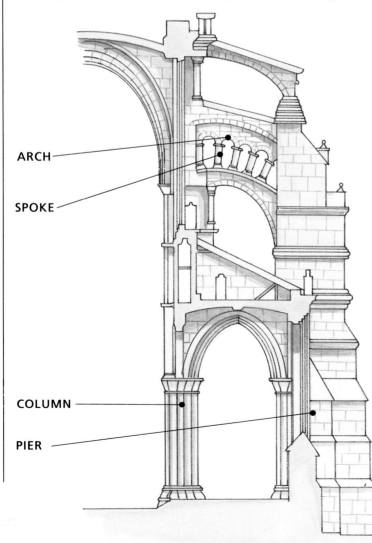

ARCH

SPOKE

COLUMN

PIER

ARCHES

From the ninth to the twelfth centuries AD, the architecture of Europe was in the **Romanesque** style. Like Roman arches, Romanesque arches (right) were semicircular. So the wider the arch, the higher it had to be. They also spread outwards, so they had to be heavily buttressed.

Pointed Gothic arches (right) could be any height and width. The steeper sides carried more of the weight directly down to the ground. This way the arches spread less and needed less buttressing.

Flying buttresses

To solve this problem, the flying buttress was invented. These structures took the pressure off the cathedral walls and carried it, through arches, to a pier and down to the ground. This allowed the walls to be thinner and to have large, stained glass windows to let in more light. Early flying buttresses, like those at Chartres, had spokes and heavy columns for extra support, but later flying buttresses became more delicate.

Chartres Cathedral is surrounded by flying buttresses like this, which carry the weight from the vaults above.

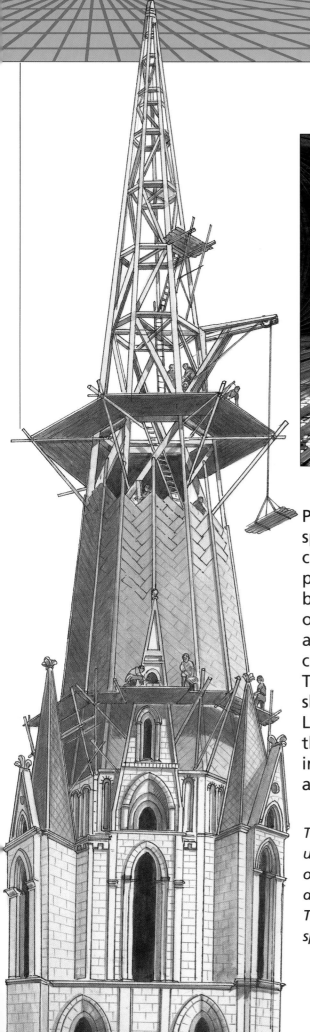

Towering spires

People hoped that the tall spires on the tops of their new churches would carry their prayers to heaven. Spires were built over the center of a church or on top of its towers. First, a wooden framework was constructed using scaffolding. Then it was covered with metal sheets to make it weatherproof. Like the rest of the building, the spires were decorated with intricate carvings of animals and plants, called **crockets.**

The south spire of Chartres Cathedral under construction. The plain octagonal south spire was built during the early thirteenth century. The taller and more ornate north spire was not built until 1507.

King's College Chapel in Cambridge, England was built between 1446 and 1515. It is famous for its huge, fan-vaulted ceiling. The vaults are supported by arched ribs that sprout from each pillar like the folds of a giant fan.

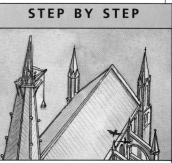

8 The roof is covered with lead sheets to make it waterproof. The spire is built from wood and covered with lead.

37

Modern Religious Buildings

For thousands of years, stone and wood were the most widely used building materials. But new materials like steel, and new ways of producing older materials like glass and concrete, have given architects the freedom to create religious buildings in exciting new styles.

Modern materials

Stone can support weight from above. But modern building materials such as iron and steel can support weight that hangs underneath them. New techniques allow concrete to be reinforced with steel rods, molded at a factory and bolted together later at a building site. Glass can be rolled into huge sheets and strengthened with plastic or wire mesh.

The role of computers

Architects of modern religious buildings have other new tools, too. They can program a computer to help them work out the best way to build a new building and the best materials to use. They can even "walk around" inside 3-D, **virtual reality** images before the foundations are laid.

In 1950, the French architect Le Corbusier designed the chapel of Notre-Dame du Haut in Ronchamp, France. It is built of reinforced concrete, and its curved roof sits on top of thick, white walls. The church is filled with colored light from stained-glass windows.

STEEL RIBS

RONCHAMP

DELHI

CASABLANCA

New ideas

A large number of religious buildings have been built during the twentieth century. Many replaced churches that were destroyed during the two **World Wars**. Some were built by architects who used new technology and materials in the old, classical styles. Others were designed by architects who wanted to use the new materials in new-style buildings. But, whatever style or materials they choose, today's architects design religious buildings for the same reason as the ancients did, as a place to worship.

The Hassan II Mosque in Casablanca was opened in 1989 to celebrate the 60th birthday of King Hassan II of Morocco. It is a traditional mosque but was built using modern technology. The roof of the prayer hall slides back to make an open-air courtyard. The **minaret** *is the tallest in the world.*

CONCRETE, GLASS, AND MARBLE "PETALS" 112 FEET (34M) HIGH

The stunning **Baha'i** *Temple in Delhi, India, represents a lotus blossom. It was designed by Fariburz Sahba and took 12 years to build. It opened in 1987.*

STEP BY STEP

9 Finally the windows are glazed, the floor tiled, the doors hung, and the bells hoisted into the tower. The cathedral is complete.

Pyramid and Temple Facts

PYRAMID POWER

About 60 pyramids were built in Ancient Egypt between 2500 and 1500 BC. Each pyramid took 20-30 years to build and employed about 70,000 men for part of the year, and another 10,000 skilled stonemasons all the time.

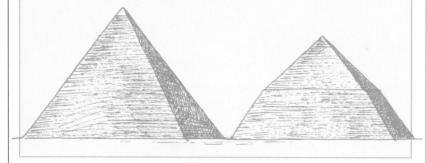

MALI MOSQUE

In Africa, people still use mud for building because it is easily available and dries quickly in the hot climate. The world's largest building made from **adobe** (mud mixed with straw) is the Great Mosque at Djenne in Mali, West Africa. It was completed in 1907.

TALL TALES

The staircases of the Maya pyramids in Central America became smaller and narrower towards the top. This created an optical illusion that made the pyramids look taller and more impressive than they really were.

ROMAN RINGS

The greatest Christian church in the world is St. Peter's in Rome. It was begun in 1506 and took 181 years to build. Much of it was designed by Michelangelo. With a 452 foot- (138m-) height and a 157 foot- (48m-) width, its dome is the largest ever built. The dome is ringed by seven huge iron chains to prevent it from spreading.

BIG BANG

The Parthenon in Athens, Greece, was built nearly 2500 years ago. This temple later became a church and then a mosque. In the seventeenth century, ammunition was stored there during a war between Turkey and Venice. In 1687 the ammunition exploded, leaving the temple in ruins.

SHINY SPIRE

Queen Shinsawbu was the first Burmese ruler to cover the stupa of the Shwe Dagon Pagoda with gold leaf. She weighed 88 pounds (40kg) and ordered the same weight of gold to be used. Later rulers regilded the stupa with even larger amounts of gold.

BURNING BUILDING

King David made Jerusalem the capital city of Israel. In the tenth century BC, his son, Solomon, decided to build a great temple there where all Jews could worship God. In about 597 BC King Solomon's Temple was burned down by the Babylonians, leaving no trace.

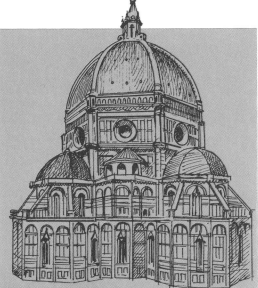

DOME DUEL

When the cathedral in Florence, Italy was constructed in the fourteenth and fifteenth centuries, no one was sure how to build a dome with a 138 foot- (42m-) width. Two architects were chosen. Brunelleschi wanted to work on his own, so he pretended to be ill until it became obvious that Ghiberti was not good enough to do the job.

HARD LABOR

The Pyramid of the Sun in Teotihuacán, Mexico, took 3,000 men 30 years to build. They had no metal tools, no wheels or machines, and did not use pack animals. The only sharp blades they had were made of obsidian, a natural form of glass.

41

Time Chart

Follow the progress of pyramids and temples through history. This time chart lists key buildings and when they were built.

c stands for circa, which means "about." It is used with dates that may not be accurate.

BC

c 15,000
Stone Age people paint animal scenes on the walls of cave at Lascaux, France.

c 7000
Early farmers build houses and shrines at Çatal Hüyük, Turkey.

c 3600
Stone Age people begin to build stone temples at Ggantija on the island of Gozo, Malta.

c 3500
Sumerians build the first ziggurat, the White Temple, at Uruk in modern-day Iraq.

c 3400
Ancient Egyptians build first mastaba tombs using mounds of sun-dried bricks.

c 2800
Work begins on Stonehenge monument, England.

c 2650
Pharaoh Zoser's Step Pyramid built by the architect Imhotep at Saqqara, Egypt.

c 2615
First true pyramid constructed for Pharaoh Sneferu in Dahshûr, Egypt.

c 2550
Great Pyramid built for Pharaoh Khufu in Giza, Egypt.

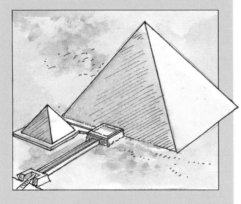

c 2340
Pyramid Texts painted on the chambers of the Pyramid of Unas in Saqqara, Egypt.

c 2100
Ziggurat built in the Sumerian city of Ur by King Ur-Nammu.

c 1600
Main work on Stonehenge, England begins.

c 1400
Tomb of Tutankhamen cut in the rockface of the Valley of the Kings, Egypt.

c 1250
Temple of Abu Simbel, Nubia, built for Pharaoh Ramses II.

c 1012
King Solomon's temple built in Jerusalem, Israel.

c 585
The first Shwe Dagon Pagoda built in Burma.

c 580
King Nebuchadrezzar builds Hanging Gardens and Tower of Babel in Babylon.

c 490
Temple of Aphaia built in Aegina, Greece.

c 447
The Parthenon built on the Acropolis at Athens, Greece.

c 100
Great Serpent Burial Mound built at Hillsboro, Ohio, by the Adena culture.

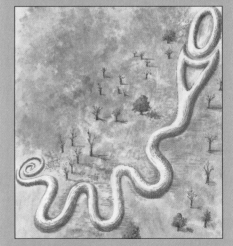

19
Maison Carrée built by the Romans at Nîmes, France.

AD

c 50
Ajanta Caves, Buddhist rock-cut temples, built in India.

100
Pyramid of the Sun built at Teotihuacán, Mexico.

120
Pantheon built in Rome, Italy.

330
First Church of St. Peter built in Rome, Italy.

c 360
The Caves of the Thousand Buddhas founded in Tun-huang, China.

532
Work begins on the church of Hagia Sophia in the city of Constantinople, now Istanbul.

539
Church of Sant' Apollinare in Classe, Ravenna, Italy, built on the site of the saint's grave.

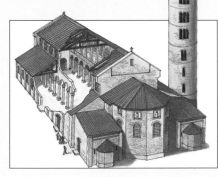

615
The Temple of the Inscriptions built at Palenque by the Maya King Pacal.

1120
Monks carve Christian verses on Externsteine caves in Germany.

1134
Work started on the first Chartres Cathedral, France.

c 1150
Angkor Wat built by the Khmer people in Cambodia.

1194
Chartres Cathedral rebuilt in the Gothic style.

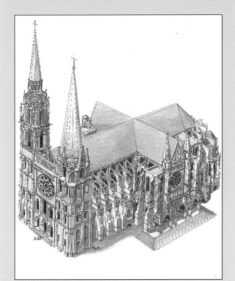

1296
Work started on Florence Cathedral, Italy.

1420
Dome of Florence Cathedral, Italy built in the Renaissance style by Brunelleschi.

1446
Work begins on King's College Chapel at the University of Cambridge, England.

1506
Work begins in Rome, Italy, on new St. Peter's to replace the fourth-century church.

1600s
The Nayak Kings build the temple complex at Madurai, southern India.

1768
Present Shwe Dagon Pagoda built by King Hsinbyushin on the sixth-century site.

1907
Great Mosque at Djenne, Mali, West Africa, finished.

1950
Church of Notre-Dame du Haut built at Ronchamp, northeast France.

1987
Baha'i Temple in Delhi, India, completed.

1989
Hassan II Mosque in Casablanca, Morocco, completed.

From Start to Finish

On these two pages, you can follow the Step by Step stories in the bottom right-hand corner of each double page from start to finish.

BUILDING A PYRAMID

1 The pharaoh's architects draw diagrams and make calculations to work out the best size and shape for the new pyramid.

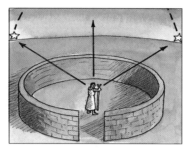

2 Priests use the top of a wall to follow a star's east to west path. The midpoint is north, the way the pyramid faces.

3 The site is leveled and a grid of channels cut and filled with water. The rock is cut back to the water level, to make it flat.

4 Pyramid stones are cut from a quarry. Wood is wedged into the rock and made wet. The wet wood swells and splits the stone.

5 The stone blocks are squared and made smooth. Then men use levers, ropes, and sledges on rollers to move them.

6 Next, men drag the sledges to the pyramid and pull the stones up a massive ramp over 1 mile (1.5 km) long.

7 A space is left near the center of the pyramid for the burial chamber. The pharaoh's sarcophagus is lowered in from above.

8 A huge granite capstone is laid at the top of the pyramid. The rest of the pyramid is covered with polished white limestone.

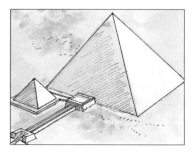

9 The Mortuary Temple, the Valley Temple, and the causeway that links them complete the great pyramid complex.

BUILDING A CATHEDRAL

1 Plans are drawn up by the architect and shown to the bishop and chapter. They decide when the building can begin.

2 Stone masons begin cutting the stone blocks for the walls, piers, and flying buttresses of the new cathedral.

3 Laborers dig holes for the foundations and the crypt. These are lined with gravel, then stone blocks are laid on the top.

4 As the piers and walls rise, the laborers build scaffolding with wooden poles. They use cranes to pull up the stone blocks.

5 The window stones are cut in shapes using wood templates. Then they are laid out on the ground to make sure they fit together.

6 Wood forms are made to support the arches. When the last stone is in place, the forms can be removed.

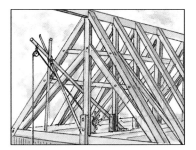

7 The triangular roof trusses are made on the ground, then taken apart, hoisted into position with a crane, and reassembled.

8 The roof is covered with lead sheets to make it waterproof. The spire is built from wood and covered with lead.

9 Finally the windows are glazed, the floor tiled, the doors hung, and the bells hoisted into the tower. The cathedral is complete.

45

Glossary

adobe A mixture of mud and straw that is dried in the sun and used for building.

aggregate Rubble added to cement and lime to give bulk to concrete.

apse A semicircular room at the end of a church or temple, often containing a shrine.

architect A person who designs a building, both inside and out.

astrologer A person who tries to predict the future by looking at the stars and the planets.

astronomer A scientist who studies the movements of the stars and planets.

Baha'i Of the Baha'i faith, a religion founded in Persia, modern-day Iran, in 1863.

basilica An oblong building with an apse at one end and aisles down either side.

bluestone A standing stone brought from the Welsh mountains and erected at Stonehenge.

Bronze Age A period between the Stone Age and the Iron Age when people made tools and weapons from bronze.

Buddha The founder of the Buddhist faith, whose followers seek enlightenment.

capstone A shaped stone on top of a building.

causeway A raised pathway.

cement A powdered mixture of limestone and clay.

centering A wood framework that supports an arch while it is being built.

chapter A group of clergy who together decide how a church's money is spent.

city-state A city that governs itself, together with the surrounding countryside.

crocket A plant or animal shape carved on the stonework of Gothic buildings.

crypt A space beneath a church that is used for burials or as a chapel.

earthwork A combination of ditches and mounds dug into the earth.

flying buttress A stone support which transfers the weight of a church roof through an arch and down to the ground.

forecourt A courtyard in front of a building.

form A wood framework that shapes an arch as it is built.

frieze A horizontal, decorated band around a building, often at the top.

gilded Covered with gold.

gopuram A decorated tower at the entrance to a Hindu temple.

Gothic Of the style of European church architecture used from the twelfth to the sixteenth centuries, featuring pointed arches, flying buttresses, and rib vaults.

granite Hard rock formed when hot, liquid rock from inside the Earth solidifies on the surface.

Hinduism The main religion of India, whose followers believe in many gods.

hypostyle hall A hall with a roof supported by many columns.

Ice Age A period about 15,000 years ago when the polar ice caps reached almost to the Equator.

jade A hard, green, semiprecious stone.

keystone The central stone at the top of an arch.

lime A chemical composed of calcium, oxygen, and hydrogen.

limestone Chalky rock made of calcium, carbon, and oxygen and formed from ancient sea shells.

lintel A horizontal beam.

Marduk The supreme god of ancient Babylon.
memento A souvenir.
minaret A tall tower forming part of a mosque. People are called to prayer from here.
mold A hollow frame used to give shape to a soft material poured or pressed into it.
Mortuary Temple A temple where the pharaoh's last funeral ceremonies took place.
mosaics Pictures or patterns made from small squares of colored glass or tile.
mummification Preservation of a body by drying and treating with oils.

nave The central area of a church, where the congregation sits.

obelisk A tall stone column with a small top section shaped like a pyramid.
order A style of architecture.
overseer A person who checks that others are doing their job correctly.

pagan Of any religion other than Christianity, Judaism, or Islam.
pagoda A Buddhist shrine with a tiered tower.
papyrus A tall reed that grows along riverbanks.
pendentive A triangular arch with curved sides that carries the weight of a dome down to the ground.
peristyle hall A hall with no roof and surrounded by columns.
persecution Ill-treatment.
pier A stone pillar that supports an arch.
pilgrim A person who goes on a journey to a sacred place.
plumb line A string with a weight at the end, used to make sure vertical lines are straight.

pulley A device consisting of grooved wheels and used with a rope to lift heavy weights.
pumice Volcanic rock full of air bubbles.

rib vault An arched ceiling supported by thick stone arches.
Romanesque Of a European style of architecture used between the ninth and twelfth centuries and featuring round arches and vaults.

sarcophagus A stone coffin.
sarsen A huge, shaped block of sandstone erected at Stonehenge.
shrine A place of worship associated with a sacred person or object.
sphinx An Egyptian stone statue with the body of a lion and the head of a king.
Stone Age A period when people used stone tools and weapons.
stone mason A person skilled in shaping stone.
stupa A Buddhist shrine with a pointed dome.

tazoung A small Buddhist shrine.
template A full-sized wooden pattern.
terra-cotta Clay fired in a kiln to make it hard.
trefoil A shape similar to that of the three-lobed leaf of a type of clover.
truss A triangular frame that supports a roof.

virtual reality Three-dimensional moving images produced by computer.
voussoir One of the wedge-shaped stones which form an arch.

World Wars World War I (1914-1918) and World War II (1939-1945), which both involved many countries of the world.

Index

Words in **bold** appear in the glossary on pages 46 and 47.